THINGS NOT SEEN

by
Andrew Clements

Teacher Guide

Written by
Monica L. Odle

Note

The Puffin Books paperback edition, © 2002 by Andrew Clements, was used to prepare this guide. Page references may differ in other editions. Novel ISBN: 0-14-240076-9

Please note: Please assess the appropriateness of this book for the age level and maturity of your students prior to reading and discussing it with them.

ISBN-10: 1-58130-934-1
ISBN-13: 978-1-58130-934-8

To order, contact your local school supply store, or—
Novel Units, Inc.
P.O. Box 97
Bulverde, TX 78163-0097

Web site: www.novelunits.com

Lori Mammen, Editorial Director
Andrea M. Harris, Production Manager/Production Specialist
Michael Hanna, Product Development Specialist
A. Taylor Henderson, Product Development Specialist
Heather M. Marnan, Product Development Specialist
Suzanne K. Mammen, Curriculum Specialist
Gabriela Mongiello, Product Development Specialist
Jill Reed, Product Development Specialist
Adrienne Speer, Production Specialist

Table of Contents

Skills and Strategies

Thinking
Brainstorming, reflecting, research, Venn diagram, critical thinking, decision making, creative thinking

Comprehension
Predicting, summarizing, evaluating decisions, sequencing

Literary Elements
Cause and effect, conflict, tone, characterization, climax, figurative language, theme, point of view

Writing
Poetry, essay, report, newspaper, review, transcript, skit

Vocabulary
Definitions, context, glossary, parts of speech

Listening/Speaking
Discussion, oral presentation, interview, skit performance

Across the Curriculum
Science—transparency, technology, solar particles; Literature—Hemingway, Dickens, Vonnegut, Wells, Hawthorne, Tolkien; Music—jazz; Art—sketching, drawing, caricatures, collage; History—Greek Olympics; Other—Braille

Genre: young-adult fiction

Setting: present day Chicago, Illinois

Point of View: first person

Themes: belonging, self-discovery, family, courage, friendship, justice

Conflict: person vs. science/nature, person vs. society, person vs. person, person vs. self

Tone: reflective, intelligent, informal

Summary

After waking up one morning as an invisible person, Bobby Phillips begins a search to discover the cause of his invisibility in hopes of reversing it. Along the way, Bobby learns how to live in society as an invisible entity and befriends a blind girl named Alicia, who, ironically, is the only person who seems to be able to "see" Bobby. Together, Bobby and Alicia, along with their families, eventually discover that Bobby's condition has resulted from a malfunctioning electric blanket and an unusual cosmic occurrence. Bobby must figure out how to make himself visible again before the authorities arrest his parents due to their increasing suspicion of the strange circumstances surrounding Bobby's disappearance.

About the Author

Andrew Clements was born on May 29, 1949, in Camden, New Jersey. His parents were avid readers who passed on to their son and his siblings a love for books and reading. While Clements wrote poems and songs during his grade school and college years, he never thought about working as a professional writer until later in life. After earning his bachelor's degree at Northwestern University in Evanstown, Illinois, Clements attended the National College of Education—now called National-Louis University—to earn his MA in elementary education. He taught in Chicago for seven years before working as a songwriter in New York and as an editorial director for Alphabet Press, a publishing company now known as Picture Book Studios. Clements currently lives in Westborough, Massachusetts, with his wife, Rebecca, and his four sons.

In 1990, Clements began writing *Frindle*, his first young-adult novel. Though it was not published until 1996, this novel earned many awards, including the 1997 Christopher Award. Since beginning his writing career, Clements has authored over 50 books for children, including *The Landry News*, *The Janitor's Boy*, *The School Story*, *The Jacket*, *The Report Card*, and *Lunch Money*. His book *Things Hoped For* is a partial sequel to *Things Not Seen*, as Clements reintroduces Bobby Phillips, *Things Not Seen*'s main character, as a supporting character less central to the story's plot. Clements enjoys writing about situations surrounding school because school is such a big part of children's lives. Besides writing, Clements' hobbies include serving on the Executive Board of Directors of the Children's Book Council and traveling to schools to share his love of books and reading with students around the country.

Sources (active at time of publication):
www.edupaperback.org/showauth.cfm?authid=48
www.eduplace.com/kids/tnc/mtai/clements.html
www.andrewclements.com/biography.shtml

Characters

Bobby Phillips: 15-year-old boy who wakes up one morning to find himself invisible

Emily Phillips: Bobby's mother; professor of literature at the University of Chicago

David Phillips: Bobby's father; scientist who studies atoms

Alicia Van Dorn: 15-year-old blind girl whom Bobby befriends at the library; helps Bobby try to figure out how to reverse his invisibility

Dr. Leo Van Dorn: Alicia's father; professor of astronomy at the University of Chicago; helps Bobby's dad theorize about Bobby's invisibility

Julia Van Dorn: Alicia's mother; left her job to care for Alicia full time following Alicia's blindness; overly protective of her daughter since Alicia became blind

Mrs. Trent: the Phillips' nosy neighbor

Dr. Sarah Fleming: doctor at Presbyterian St. Luke's Hospital who is responsible for making sure an adult is caring for Bobby at home while his parents recover from a car accident

Aunt Ethel: Bobby's great aunt who lives in Florida; Bobby's parents falsely claim that she is watching Bobby while they are in the hospital, and later, that Bobby is visiting her in Florida indefinitely

Martha Pagett: officer at the State Department of Children and Family Services; believes Bobby's disappearance is suspicious and threatens to imprison Bobby's parents if they are uncooperative in her search for Bobby

Charles Clark: the Phillips' lawyer

Amber Carson: woman at Sears whom Alicia talks to on the phone about the electric blanket; Bobby uses her terminal to access information about customers who returned blankets

Sheila Borden: young woman in her 20s who was affected by an electric blanket like Bobby's; ran away from her parents' home after she became invisible; now lives in Florida and designs Web sites

Initiating Activities

1. Brainstorming: Write the word "invisible" on an attribute web for the class to see (see page 6 of this guide). Have students brainstorm about being invisible and how it would affect a person's everyday life. Discuss the repercussions of discovering how to make people invisible and the effect this would have on society.

2. Research: Have students research different causes of blindness and report their findings to the class. Discuss how being born blind and developing blindness later in life might affect a person in different ways.

3. Prereading: Discuss as a class why the author titled his book *Things Not Seen*. What will the book be about? What issues will it raise? Then have students complete the Getting the "Lay of the Land" activity on page 7 of this guide.

4. Prediction: Have students begin the Prediction Chart on page 8 of this guide. Students should continue this activity as they read the novel.

5. Reflection: Have students consider whether they would rather be seen or heard. Then have students write about their decision, including specific reasons for their choice.

Vocabulary Activities

1. Speed Speech: Divide the class into pairs. One student in each pair is given a set of 20 vocabulary words. Start a timer as students read the vocabulary word aloud to their partners. The partner must quickly identify the part of speech for that vocabulary word as it is used in the book. The first student to give the correct parts of speech for all 20 words is the winner of round one. Then the other student in each pair is given a different set of 20 vocabulary words. These students then call out the words to their partners. Again, the first student to correctly identify the parts of speech for all 20 words is the winner for round two. Have a run-off round between the two winners where the teacher asks each student to identify the part of speech for ten new vocabulary words. Use the same set of words for each student in the run-off round, making sure the second student cannot hear the first student's responses.

2. Sentence-by-Sentence: Have students brainstorm about introductory sentences that could be used to start a story. Once students have chosen an introductory sentence, they should pass around a blank sheet of paper with the starter sentence written at the top. Each student must add a sentence to the story that correctly uses one vocabulary word. After each class member has contributed to the story, have a volunteer read the story aloud.

3. Writing: Have students write a free verse poem about being invisible or blind. Students should use at least eight vocabulary words from the book.

4. Glossary: Using a computer spreadsheet or database, have students create a glossary of vocabulary words found in the book. Each entry should include the word, its part of speech, the definition as the word is used in the book, the page number on which the word can be found, and an antonym of the word where appropriate.

5. Vocabulary Stump: Divide the class into equal groups. Assign each group a set of 30 vocabulary words. The first person in the group will randomly select a word. The rest of the team will collaborate—one person will read out the definition of the word while the rest of the team members give false, but plausible, definitions for the word. The first person must then select which definition is correct. Play proceeds to the right. Players receive one point for each correctly chosen definition. No points are awarded if the player chooses an incorrect definition. The player with the most points is the winner. If time allows, have the winner from each group play a championship round while the rest of the class observes and participates by providing false definitions. The teacher should read all of the contrived, as well as the actual, definitions during the championship round.

Attribute Web

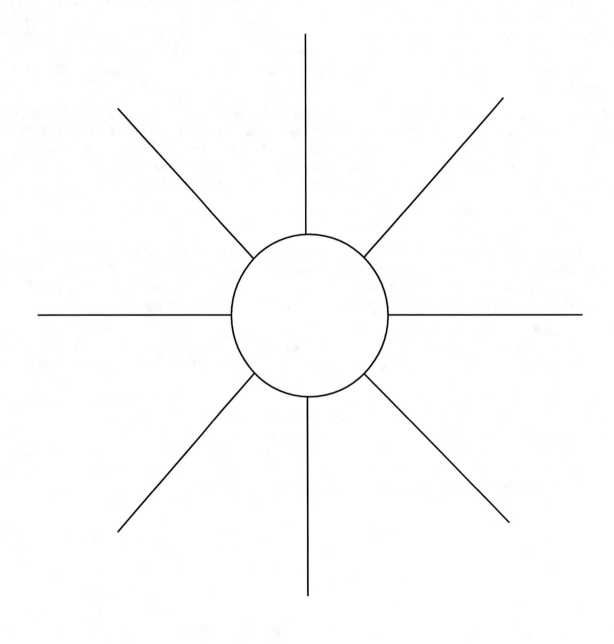

Getting the "Lay of the Land"

Directions: Prepare for reading by answering the following short-answer questions.

1. Who is the author?

   _____

2. What does the title suggest to you about the book?

   _____

   _____

   _____

   _____

3. When was the book first copyrighted?

   _____

4. How many pages are there in the book?

   _____

5. Thumb through the book. Read three pages—one from near the beginning, one from near the middle, and one from near the end. What predictions can you make about the book?

   _____

   _____

   _____

   _____

   _____

6. What does the cover suggest to you about the book?

   _____

   _____

   _____

   _____

Prediction Chart

What characters have we met so far?	What is the conflict in the story?	What are your predictions?	Why did you make these predictions?

Figurative Language

Simile	Personification	Metaphor

Character Web

Directions: Complete the attribute web below by filling in information specific to a character in the book.

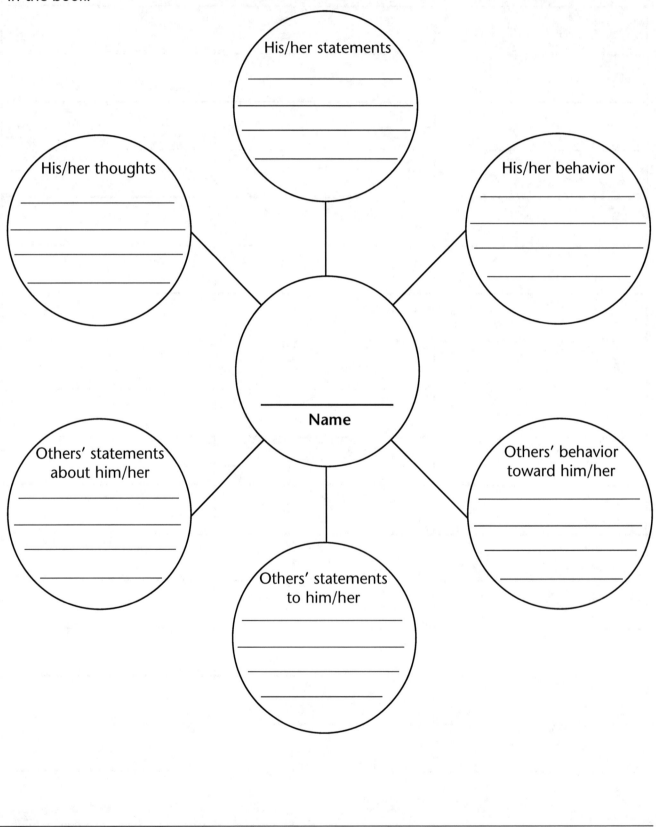

Story Map

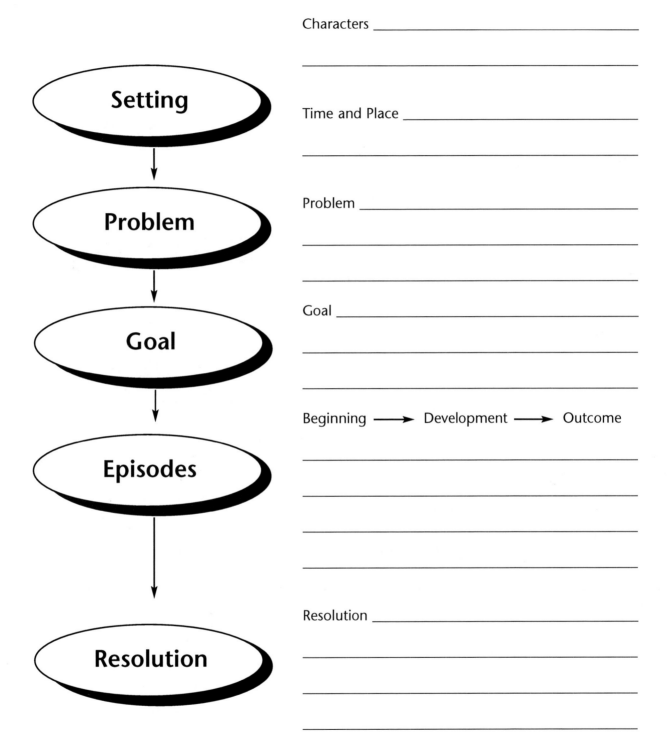

Setting

Problem

Goal

Episodes

Resolution

Characters _____

_____

Time and Place _____

_____

Problem _____

_____

_____

Goal _____

_____

_____

Beginning ⟶ Development ⟶ Outcome

_____

_____

_____

_____

Resolution _____

_____

_____

_____

Cause/Effect Chart

Directions: Make a flow chart to show decisions a character made, the decisions s/he could have made, and the result(s) of each. (Use your imagination to speculate on the results of decisions the character could have made.)

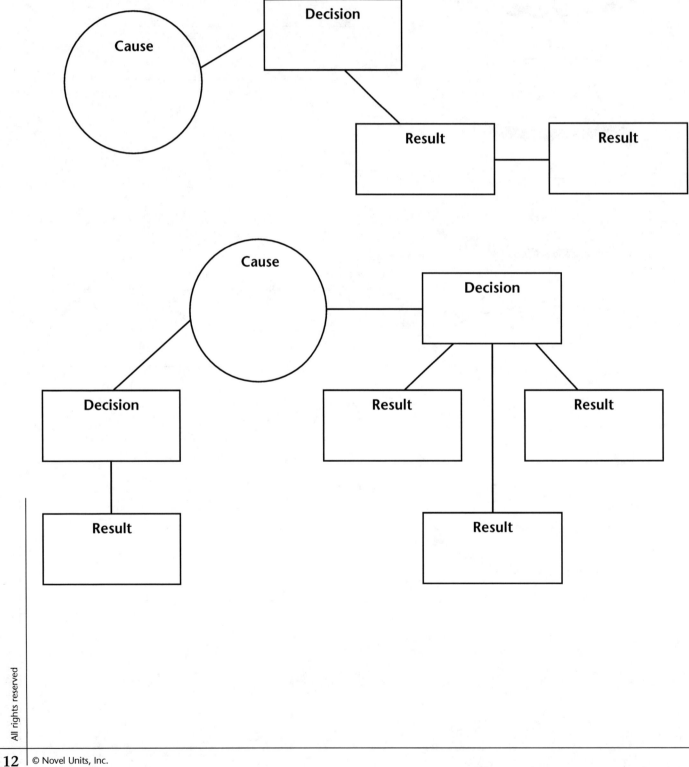

12 | © Novel Units, Inc.

Venn Diagram

Bobby   **Alicia**

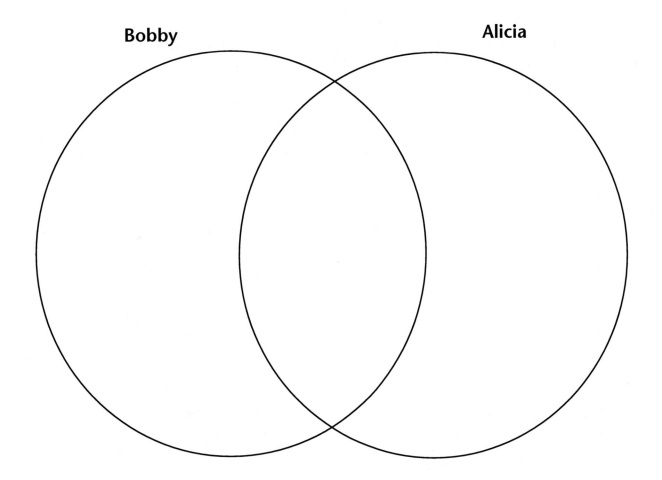

Chapters 1–3, pp. 1–28

Fifteen-year-old Bobby Phillips wakes up one morning to find he is invisible. After he and his parents overcome the shock of this new phenomenon, they begin to discuss how it might have happened and what they might do to reverse the situation. Bobby leaves the house bundled in winter wear and visits the library, where he stashes his clothes and walks around observing others without being seen. On his way out of the library, Bobby collides with a female student, and in the process, knocks off his scarf. Fearing that his cover has been blown and his secret divulged, Bobby is relieved when he realizes that the young girl is blind.

Vocabulary
banister (2)
motto (3)
theory (4)
phenomenon (4)
civil (7)
fold (9)
tuition (10)
potential (13)
refraction (14)
density (16)
vital (19)
disoriented (22)
dimension (26)

Discussion Questions

1. Discuss why you think the author chose to write this book as a first-person narrative rather than in third person. *(Answers will vary. Note that hearing Bobby's voice tell the story makes it easier for readers to relate to what he is feeling and experiencing.)*

2. How do Bobby and his parents respond to Bobby's invisibility? Do you think their responses are realistic? Why or why not? How might you respond if you woke up one morning as an invisible person? *(Bobby is shocked and disturbed and decides to ask his parents for help. At first, Bobby's parents think Bobby is trying to trick them. Bobby convinces his parents that he is telling them the truth by swigging down a glass of orange juice while in his invisible state. Upon witnessing this, Mr. and Mrs. Phillips are astonished and upset. Bobby doesn't know how to act, and his dad starts hypothesizing about what might have caused the invisibility. Bobby's mother seems most upset in the beginning and thinks they should call the family doctor. Answers will vary. pp. 1–7)*

3. What does Bobby's dad think they must be experiencing? Is this a real phenomenon or one made up for the purpose of the book? *(a "visible light anomaly"; Such anomalies are observed by scientists, but no one has ever been reported invisible due to one. Unusual light activity is usually observed in space. p. 4)*

4. As his parents try to solve his dilemma, Bobby thinks that the situation becomes all "about them" (p. 9). Do you agree or disagree with Bobby's point of view? *(Answers will vary.)*

5. To what does Mr. Phillips compare Bobby's invisibility? Do you think this concept helps clarify what has happened to Bobby's body? *(Mr. Phillips compares Bobby to the Stealth Bomber. Bobby is invisible to the human eye just as the Stealth Bomber is invisible to radar. While both are unseen in different situations, they both actually exist. Answers will vary. pp. 12–13)*

6. Do you approve of the way Bobby treats his parents after he becomes invisible? Why or why not? Do you approve of Mr. and Mrs. Phillips' decision to leave Bobby alone the afternoon after he wakes up as an invisible person? Explain your answer. *(Answers will vary. Suggestion: Some students may feel Bobby has a right to be rude to his parents because he is going through a difficult situation. Others may think that he doesn't have the right to snap at his parents because they are supportive and concerned about him even though they currently do not know how to help him. Also, some students may think Bobby's parents should act as normal as possible so as to detract attention from Bobby's invisibility. Others may agree with Bobby that he should not have been left alone, even if he was asleep. throughout, pp. 18–19)*

7. What does Bobby decide to do while his parents are gone? Why? Do you think this is a wise decision? What would you have done if you were in Bobby's place? *(Bobby decides to go to the library because he wants to experience life outside his house as an invisible being just in case he wakes up and is visible again. Answers will vary. p. 20)*

8. Why is Bobby glad that the girl in the library runs over his toe with the chair? *(It reminds him that the rules are different when he is invisible. He has to be careful. If something happens to him while no one can see him, no one will be able to help him. pp. 23–26)*

9. **Prediction:** Do you think Bobby will bump into the blind girl again?

Supplementary Activities

1. Figurative Language: Figurative language conveys meaning through the use of analogy. Begin making a list of the figurative language in the novel using the chart on page 9 of this guide. Examples: **Similes**—"she freaks, like she's grabbed a lizard" (p. 5); "house is like a library" (p. 15); "moving…like a gray caterpillar" (p. 16); **Metaphors**—bones: tuna salad (p. 5); students at the library: drones in a beehive (p. 23); **Personification**—"shower curtain jump" (p. 2)

2. Writing/Science: Bobby's father explains that because Bobby's shadow is visible when Bobby is close to a solid surface, he is not totally transparent even though he cannot be seen (p. 14). Write a paragraph explaining the difference between being invisible and being transparent.

3. Literature: Research the works of Ernest Hemingway and Charles Dickens. Select the author whose books you would most like to read. Write a report about the author you selected, including what intrigues you about his life or writing.

4. Music: Conduct historical research about the jazz scene in Chicago in the early to mid-twentieth century. Report on one aspect of jazz music in Chicago during that era. (Students may report on artists, such as Louis Armstrong or Dr. Andrew [Andy] Goodrich. They may also find information about the music itself or women's role in jazz during that time. One starting point for research could be the Chicago Jazz Archives located at www.lib.uchicago.edu/e/su/cja/artists.html. [Active at time of publication.])

Chapters 4–7, pp. 29–60

Bobby apologizes to the blind girl he runs into while leaving the library. At home, he gets angry with his father for leaving him alone during the day. Bobby's father tries to reconcile with Bobby and then leaves to pick up Bobby's mother at the university campus. Bobby settles down for a nap and awakens to find that his parents have been in a car accident. Bobby sneaks into the hospital to visit his parents. Mrs. Phillips, in an effort to keep Bobby's condition a secret, tells the hospital doctor that a distant relative has come in from out of town to care for Bobby while she and Mr. Phillips are in the hospital. Back at his house, Bobby finds himself afraid of being home alone at night.

Vocabulary

beveled (31)
fatal (32)
impacts (36)
concussion (38)
arctic (45)
complexion (59)
fleece (59)

Discussion Questions

1. How do you know Bobby likes the girl he runs into at the library? *(He spends time thinking about which author could do the best job of describing her pretty face. He says that Hemingway wouldn't do her justice "because he'd say something like, 'It was a pretty face.' And that wouldn't be enough." p. 29)*

2. When Bobby yells at his father, do you think he really means everything he says or is he just trying to make his parents feel guilty so he won't get in trouble for leaving the house? Explain your answer. *(Answers will vary. pp. 32–33)*

3. Why does the author have Bobby's parents get into an auto accident the same day Bobby finds himself invisible? Do you think this writing choice adds or detracts from the story? Explain. *(Answers will vary. Students might say that allowing Bobby to be on his own for several days will give the author room to let Bobby experiment with his invisibility more freely. It also adds to the tension of the story. pp. 34–36)*

4. As Bobby sits at home after talking to Dr. Fleming, he begins to feel overwhelmed with the lies his parents must tell to keep his invisibility a secret. Do you approve of all the lies the Phillips family is telling? Why or why not? Do you think there is ever a time when it is okay to lie, or are lies always wrong? *(Answers will vary. pp. 40–41)*

5. Why do you think Bobby feels compelled to visit his parents in the hospital even though the doctor tells him they are fine? *(Answers will vary. At one point, he says he should go because that is what family does. Later, he admits that he is not totally convinced he can trust what the doctor told him. Perhaps he feels guilty for making his parents feel bad about leaving him alone, and in some way, feels responsible for the accident. Perhaps he simply wants to talk to his mom to make sure they have their story straight about a caretaker. pp. 40–49)*

6. What things does Bobby worry about once he returns home from the hospital? Discuss which things he should and should not be concerned about. *(Answers will vary. He is worried about Mrs. Trent seeing him, his mom not answering the phone, and simply being in an empty house. The fear of his house is irrational, but his worry about Mrs. Trent suspecting his invisibility is something about which he should be mindful. pp. 53–59)*

7. **Prediction:** Will Mrs. Trent discover that something is strange about Bobby? Will Bobby's parents both really be okay?

Supplementary Activities

1. Figurative Language: Continue adding to your chart. Examples: **Similes**—"mouth tastes like copper" (p. 30); "piercing...like porcupine quills" (p. 33); "feel as if I've been punched in the stomach" (p. 46); **Personification**—"heart...drumming" (p. 30); "words...hit" (p. 33); "big red Jeep beat her up" (p. 39); "fear begins to crawl" (p. 56); "system will shriek" (p. 56); "dread is oozing" (p. 58)

2. Art: Draw a sketch or caricature of what Bobby looks like when he shows up at the hospital completely covered and with glasses on at night. Consider how others react to his appearance as you draw.

3. Writing/Poetry: When describing how Bobby feels during his first night at home alone, the author describes fear as if it is a person. Write a poem that personifies fear and describes the feelings fear can create within a person.

Chapters 8–11, pp. 61–93

Bobby describes his life and decides to go out rather than continue to sit at home doing nothing. He visits his school during dismissal and then goes to the library where he sees the blind girl in a soundproof room. He ventures in and begins talking with her. Bobby escorts the girl, Alicia, home, but during their walk, Alicia discovers that Bobby is naked. To prevent her from thinking he is just a creepy guy looking to prey on an innocent blind girl, Bobby tells Alicia the truth about his invisibility. Alicia promises not to tell anyone about Bobby's situation.

Vocabulary
vintage (62)
spectrometer (62)
generate (63)
invalid (63)
gander (65)
beanie (70)
mill (72)
terminals (78)
demented (80)
detour (83)
wonk (91)

Discussion Questions

1. In Chapter 8, Bobby describes his life. He also ponders what his peers would think of being invisible. What do you think you would do if you were invisible? Would you be like Bobby? Or would you do the things Bobby imagines his friends suggesting? Why? *(Answers will vary. Note: Bobby thinks his friends would encourage him to become a spy or peek in the girls' locker room. Bobby explains that doing these things isn't a reality for him because his condition won't just go away—he will have to live with the consequences of any action he takes, especially if someone discovers what has happened to him. pp. 61–68)*

2. Bobby imagines he is a Greek warrior while walking around his neighborhood naked. What does this tell you about his character? What does it show about humanity when Bobby observes how people behave when they don't think anyone is watching them? *(Answers will vary. Bobby is brave to go out in public naked, particularly because it is cold and would seem socially awkward to be naked in public. He is also a bit dramatic, which is particularly noted when he continues to refer to himself as a Greek warrior and references how Greek warriors behave in situations such as his. Bobby is able to see people in a more authentic way by watching them when they think no one is looking. It shows how often people put on a façade to impress or be accepted by others, even if it means not behaving in a way that is true to who they are. pp. 69–73)*

3. What does Alicia's response to Bobby's question about her blindness tell you about her character? Why do you think so? Why do you think the author includes this dialogue? *(Answers will vary. At first, the girl is defensive, and then she softens and becomes more sarcastic.*

She seems willing to talk about her blindness, but it seems she is still bitter about her impairment. The author may have included this conversation to illustrate how Bobby feels but in the voice of a different character. Bobby, given time, could become bitter about having an impairment forced upon him that would upset his entire life. pp. 77–79)

4. Do you think Bobby should have told Alicia that he is invisible? Why or why not? *(Answers will vary. Some students may think it is good that he has a friend besides his parents he can talk with, or they may understand his desire to be liked by Alicia and not thought of as a deviant of some sort. Others may think it is too risky and that he should have left her thinking he was some creep. pp. 84–93)*

5. **Prediction:** Will Bobby's parents find out he told someone he was invisible? Will Alicia keep Bobby's secret?

Supplementary Activities

1. Figurative Language: Continue adding to your chart. Examples: **Similes**—"metal bars feel like icicles" (p. 71); "girls glide down the front steps...like airplanes in formation" (p. 72); "shakes my hand like a puppy shaking a rag" (p. 90); **Metaphors**—Bobby: Human Hidden Camera (p. 70); Bobby: a lone Greek warrior (p. 70); Alicia's white cane: magic wand (p. 84)

2. History: Bobby mentions that the ancient Greeks went to battle naked. Besides going into battle naked, they also competed in some sports without wearing any clothes. Research the first Olympic Games, which were held in Greece. Give a report about the events of the first Olympics and the people who competed in them.

3. Creative Thinking: Using an attribute web (see page 6 of this guide), brainstorm a list of other impossibilities, besides invisibility, that you would have a difficult time believing.

Chapters 12–15, pp. 94–125

Bobby and Alicia become friends. Bobby's mother returns home from the hospital. While visiting Alicia at the library one day, Bobby reveals his identity to Alicia's father. Bobby's parents come to terms with his decision to trust the Van Dorn family. Bobby starts recording everything he can remember about the few days before he became invisible. Bobby's school, as well as the Department of Children and Family Services, become suspicious of Bobby's lengthy absence from school, and a caseworker visits the Phillips household looking for Bobby.

Vocabulary
threshold (94)
patented (97)
hovering (102)
maladjustment (112)
commuting (112)
infrared (114)
sleuthing (116)
truancy (119)
jackbooted (121)
perjury (124)
fugitive (124)

Discussion Questions

1. Why do you think Bobby trusts Alicia to be his friend while he is invisible rather than a friend he already has from school or his neighborhood? *(Answers will vary. Suggestion: Alicia understands how Bobby feels because her blindness makes her feel like an outsider, too. His other friends might be prone to tell a teacher or parent what happened, which would violate the need for secrecy which Bobby's parents feel is so important. pp. 94–99)*

2. Bobby is frustrated that his parents don't trust him to make decisions about his own life. Do you agree with Bobby that he should be able to tell anyone he wants about his invisibility and do anything he likes while he is invisible, regardless of what his parents tell him to do? Explain your answer. *(Answers will vary. Note that just after leaving the argument with his mother,*

Bobby runs outside into very cold weather. It is ironic because he had just talked about being able to make good decisions for himself, yet he calls himself stupid in the next moment. Also, note that sometimes parents have the capacity to think ahead better than young adults because they have more life experience. Also note that Bobby's parents tell him what to do because they love him and want what is best for him. A government agency might tell Bobby what to do but may not have Bobby's best interests in mind. pp. 100–102)

3. Why do you think Alicia is dressed as though she is going on a date when she has only spoken with Bobby in person once? *(Answers will vary. Note that most of Alicia's friends deserted her after she became blind. Bobby may be one of the only people who has tried to befriend her in a long time. She may also have a crush on Bobby after talking with him. p. 102)*

4. What is interesting about the way Alicia became blind compared to how Bobby became invisible? *(Both incidents happened in the middle of the night, and both people were fine the night before when they went to bed. They both woke up in a different type of darkness—Bobby's body was gone, and Alicia's inability to see made her feel as if it was still night. Also, as a result of becoming blind or invisible, they ended up being separated from their friends and their "normal" lives. After discovering what happened, both were upset and eventually felt like their futures had disappeared— particularly the likelihood of marrying or having children or a career. In both cases, as well, there seems to be no way to reverse or cure the condition. pp. 104–107)*

5. After hearing what Alicia has to say about Nancy, how would you define a true friend? Is every friend a true friend? Explain your answer. *(Answers will vary. Note how all of Alicia's other friends deserted her after she became blind. Also note how Nancy's presence brought so much comfort to Alicia. You may point out how Nancy's selflessness and service to Alicia set her apart from the other people Alicia knew. Her willingness to serve and comfort Alicia had nothing to do with Nancy's personal social status or personal needs. p. 107)*

6. Why do you think Bobby's father is okay with Bobby letting the entire Van Dorn family in on "The Bobby Story"? *(Answers will vary. Suggestion: He may feel truly overwhelmed, as the text states. Also note that Bobby's father seems to treat Bobby more as an adult than he did at the beginning of the story. pp. 110–112)*

7. Do you agree with Bobby that something must have caused his invisibility, or do you think it just happened without any cause? Explain your answer. *(Answers will vary. p. 115)*

8. Do you think it is realistic for so many people at Bobby's school to be so concerned about his absences? Why or why not? *(Answers will vary. pp. 116–118)*

9. **Prediction:** Will Ms. Pagett discover the truth about Bobby? Will Mr. and Mrs. Phillips suffer the consequences of being unable to produce their son?

Supplementary Activities

1. Figurative Language: Continue adding to your chart. Examples: **Similes**—"move…like an old person" (p. 100); "waves her hand as if to whisk away that idea" (p. 121); "people are like pit bulls" (p. 123); "bruises…look bright as goldfinches" (p. 123); **Metaphor**— conversation: small war (p. 121)

2. Research: Research the Braille alphabet. Design a display showing the arrangement of the dots, and share your findings with the class. Explain how blind people are able to differentiate between letters and symbols.

3. Literature: Research the works of Kurt Vonnegut and reviews or summaries of his books that are referenced on page 113 in *Things Not Seen*. Write a short essay explaining why you think Andrew Clements chose to reference this particular author or these specific works in the book. (Note: Vonnegut's writings often deal with scientific drama, and some short stories in *Welcome to the Monkey House* deal with people who are not visible. Both Alicia and Bobby are children of scientists.)

Chapters 16–18, pp. 126–163

Ms. Pagett returns to the Phillips household with a warrant and three police officers. After searching the house and finding nothing, Ms. Pagett and the police officers leave with the threat that Bobby's parents could be in trouble if they do not produce Bobby in one week. Determined to do something to prevent his parents from going to jail, Bobby tries to find other invisible people based on a theory that if invisibility happened to him, it's probably happened to someone else as well. Bobby hopes that if he finds another invisible person, he might be able to better figure out how to reverse his condition and become visible again. Later, the Van Dorns join the Phillips family for dinner, where Mr. Phillips and Dr. Van Dorn deduce that the cause of Bobby's invisibility could be linked to his malfunctioning electric blanket.

Vocabulary
premises (128)
collusion (128)
jurisdiction (129)
reciprocal (129)
liable (130)
albino (136)
abduction (138)
snivel (141)
indices (145)
jargon (146)
imperceptible (150)
oscilloscope (151)
schematic (153)
capacitors (153)
transformers (153)
resistors (153)
cathode (154)
prejudice (160)

Discussion Questions

1. Do you believe that Mrs. Trent will figure out that Mrs. Phillips is fabricating her story? Why or why not? *(Answers will vary. pp. 129–130)*

2. How do you think Bobby feels when his mother tells him it is possible for her and Mr. Phillips to be arrested because Bobby is "missing"? *(Answers will vary. p. 131)*

3. What do you think of Bobby's theory that there must be other invisible people in society besides him? If they exist, how do you think Bobby will find them? *(Answers will vary. pp. 139–141)*

4. Do you think Alicia ruined her mother's life? Do you think Alicia's mother believes this? Do you think Alicia should feel guilty? *(Answers will vary. pp. 147–148)*

5. Alicia questions Bobby about why he discounts theories he reads on the Internet about the "hocus-pocus gang," or spiritual or magical beliefs of why people become invisible (p. 149). Discuss the difference between a scientific and spiritual occurrence. Is one more or less valid than the other? *(Answers will vary. Scientific occurrences tend to be proven by logic. Spiritual occurrences are usually credited to a divine being or mystical happening. In Bobby's case, he really is invisible, but there also isn't yet any scientific logic to prove how he came to be that way. When discussing validity, try to create a safe environment for students to speak freely about believing "truths" based on faith or scientific proof. pp. 149–150)*

6. After Mr. Van Dorn and Bobby's dad find a possible breakthrough with the malfunctioning electric blanket, why does Bobby get angry? *(Bobby tries to converse with them about what they are doing, but they seem to ignore him. Bobby is irritated because he came up with the idea to search his room for clues and no one paid attention to his efforts. Now that those efforts have proved fruitful, he wishes they would continue to listen to him. He also seems to want more validation from his dad for his efforts as well as more consultation as they search for the cause of his invisibility. He feels like his dad is more interested in the science of what has happened than in Bobby's wellbeing. p. 156)*

7. Do you think Bobby and Alicia would have become friends if Alicia could see and Bobby wasn't invisible? Explain. *(Answers will vary. pp. 159–161)*

8. How do you think Bobby's parents feel about Bobby being invisible? Do you think they really believe everything will be fine like they tell Bobby? *(Answers will vary. Bobby's parents do seem very concerned. Bobby's father seems intent on solving the problem, while Bobby's mother is simply trying to cope with learning to live with an invisible child. pp. 161–163)*

9. **Prediction:** Do you think the electric blanket has something to do with Bobby's invisibility? Will a solution to Bobby's problem be found before Ms. Pagett returns?

Supplementary Activities

1. Figurative Language: Continue adding to your chart. Examples: **Similes**—"[dinner party]...like a science seminar" (p. 145); "spinning out theories like madmen" (p. 146); **Personification**—"small radio has a big voice" (p. 130)

2. Literature: Read *The Invisible Man* by H.G. Wells, or read summaries and reviews of the text. Based on what you learn, compare and contrast the main character in *The Invisible Man* to Bobby Phillips. (Note: Mr. Griffin in the Wells classic is driven to pursue invisibility with the hope of it bringing him freedom and power, while Bobby Phillips did not desire invisibility, nor does he exploit it to become powerful. Both Bobby and Mr. Griffin learn that being invisible causes many difficulties in living an ordinary life, and both find themselves more as captives than free men. Griffin doesn't seem to handle his invisibility as well as Bobby, as Griffin eventually turns to violence to lash out at a society he tried to escape. Bobby simply wants to rejoin society and live a normal life.)

3. Writing: Alicia says she prefers hearing/reading books rather than watching movies she hasn't already seen. Write a poem that compares and contrasts hearing a story in book and movie form.

Chapters 19–22, pp. 164–199

Bobby theorizes that there must be other invisible people beside himself. He calls the electric blanket manufacturer to find out who else returned the blankets. When they refuse to give him the information, he and Alicia take a taxicab to the company's headquarters. While Alicia distracts the front desk, Bobby finds the information. Bobby sees Alicia smiling and laughing with employees at the company before they head home, and he feels disconnected from her in some way. Bobby begins calling the people on his list and thinks he finds a lead.

Vocabulary

azaleas (165)
illusion (165)
dictation (169)
liberty (170)
hail (172)
corridor (179)
pacemaker (181)
perimeter (183)
churning (189)
blacklisted (195)
negotiator (195)

Discussion Questions

1. Do you think Bobby will find other invisible people from the names on his list? Why do you think the company will not give Bobby a list of people who returned the blanket? *(Answers will vary. Note: Some companies keep return information private because they do not want to make it easy for the group of disgruntled consumers to join forces in a lawsuit against the company. pp. 164–168)*

2. Do you think it is wise for Bobby and Alicia to visit the Sears headquarters to get the information Bobby wants? What are the pros and cons of Bobby's plan? *(Answers will vary. Suggestions: Pros—Bobby is invisible, so he will likely not get caught stealing the information. Alicia going with him is a good decoy for Bobby. Bobby has the money to pay taxi fare both ways. Bobby will have information that may give him a lead and help him figure out how to become visible again. Cons—It is illegal to steal this confidential information. Alicia is blind, so this is risky for her, particularly because Bobby is limited in his ability to take care of her in an emergency due to his invisibility. If something happens to Bobby, no one will be able to find him again because he is invisible. Bobby and Alicia do not tell their parents about their plan, so no one will know where to look for them should something go wrong. pp. 171–173)*

3. How does the author portray Mrs. Van Dorn in the novel? *(Answers will vary. Note how the author shows her as sad and seemingly lonely, yet interesting and intelligent. Alicia feels guilty that her mother has to watch out for her now and cannot pursue the career she once enjoyed. The author also likens her to Bobby's mother, who now has more worries for her son than she did a month ago. The author portrays this through Mrs. Van Dorn's actions instead of her words. He describes her body language to inform readers about what is going on internally. pp. 174–175)*

4. Why does it bother Bobby that Alicia is so happy when talking with the Sears employees? *(Answers will vary. Suggestion: Even though Alicia is happy, Bobby realizes he is not a part of that happiness. He also realizes he will never fully understand what it is like to be blind. Even though he is invisible, he still has hopes of reversing his situation. Alicia also seems to act differently toward him after her meeting; Bobby feels like she is putting up a wall between them. Note that once Bobby learns about Alicia's meeting, he is happy she has more hope for a "normal" future, and tells her he thinks that might have been the true purpose for their adventure. pp. 185–187, 197–199)*

5. Do you think that Sheila is invisible? Why or why not? *(Answers will vary. pp. 190–194)*

6. What do you think about the way Bobby treats Alicia's mother when she asks about where Alicia was that afternoon? Do you think Bobby should have told her the truth or not? Explain. *(Answers will vary. p. 195)*

7. **Prediction:** Will Bobby's investigations make it possible for him to eventually be visible again?

Supplementary Activities

1. Figurative Language: Continue adding to your chart. Examples: **Similes**—"I'm...like a general" (p. 171); "nostrils flare like a wild pony sniffing the wind" (pp. 177–178); "[building is] still like a maze" (p. 183); "it's like this wave sweeps over me" (p. 184); **Metaphors**—idea to break into Sears: campaign, battle (p. 171); Bobby: warrior (p. 172); **Personification**—"ambulance screaming" (p. 177); "cab is crawling" (p. 186); "hair on my arms stand up" (p. 190)

2. Research: Conduct research on the Internet or interview an administrator at your school to determine what rules the government has about hiring people with disabilities. Report on your findings. Include a definition of "disabilities" when explaining the laws or acts you discover.

3. Writing: Bobby is amazed at Alicia's ability to stay interested in her surroundings even though she can't see out the windows of the taxi. Write a descriptive poem about being in a specific environment. Describe the environment without using visual references. Instead, focus on descriptions that rely on the senses of touch, sound, smell, and taste.

Chapters 23–28, pp. 200–251

Ms. Pagett continues to look for Bobby. Bobby discovers Sheila, a woman who once owned the same type of electric blanket and then became invisible. Bobby finds out the date that Sheila vanished, and Dr. Van Horn discovers that Bobby and Sheila both became invisible on dates when there was a large burst of solar particles in space. Bobby discovers the number of solar particles is very high again, and after talking to Alicia, decides to sleep with his electric blanket. The next morning, Ms. Pagett and a team of police officers arrive at the Phillips' house to find Bobby in his room—visible. Bobby celebrates with his family and Alicia, and he mails Sheila information on how to reverse her situation should she ever want to become visible again. Alicia and Bobby meet for the first time since Bobby's invisibility has been reversed. Bobby tries to kiss Alicia, but she rejects him. Later, Alicia shares a poem with Bobby that describes her true feelings for him.

Vocabulary
hologram (200)
acoustics (201)
presumed (202)
confidentiality (208)
quarks (212)
mesons (212)
interrogation (215)
parameters (218)
radiation (218)
observatory (224)
protoplasm (230)
intuition (241)

Discussion Questions

1. Why do you think the author chooses to include a dream at the beginning of Chapter 23? (*Answers will vary. Note that including the dream is a way to remind the readers of the stakes that Bobby is facing; if he does not become visible before Ms. Pagett and the other officers revisit the Phillips' home, his parents could be imprisoned. It also adds to the tension of the story by reminding readers of the short amount of time Bobby has to reverse his situation. p. 200*)

2. Do you agree with Bobby's statement that "it takes truth to find truth" (p. 203)? Explain. (*Answers will vary.*)

3. Does Shelia seem to enjoy her life? Would you like to live a life like Shelia's? Explain. (*Sheila seems content, even though she had to leave her old life behind, including her parents, friends, etc. Answers will vary. pp. 206–210*)

4. On page 211, Bobby accounts for what he knows after talking to Sheila. Are there other things he knows for which he hasn't accounted? Do you agree or disagree with his sentiment that he really has a bunch of nothing? Explain. *(Answers will vary. Note that Bobby doesn't consider the emotional aspect of finding someone else like him. Even if he can't find a way to reverse his situation, at least he has someone else who can fully understand the obstacles he must overcome to live a fairly normal life. p. 211)*

5. Why do you think the author incorporates instant messages into the text of the novel? Is this an effective way to communicate a story? Does using this format help you better relate to or understand the characters? *(Answers will vary. Note that one technique of post-modernism is to combine different elements together, such as a traditional text with dialogue and the direct text from an instant message. Using different formats can help authors communicate different sides of a character or a plot line. Answers will vary. pp. 213–214, 248–251)*

6. Bobby's dad tells him that finding another invisible person is "first-class work" (p. 216). Bobby interprets the comment as his father being proud of him. Do you think it is important to Bobby that his father is proud of him? Explain. *(Answers will vary. Note that Bobby brings up the issue of his father being proud of him. That Bobby is thinking about it shows his father's opinion of him matters. p. 216)*

7. Do you agree or disagree with Dr. Van Dorn and Mr. Phillips' thoughts that they must keep what they know about Bobby's invisibility a secret? Explain. Bobby is angry that they made a decision about him without consulting him. Do you think he has a valid argument? *(Answers will vary. Note the concept of utilitarianism—the greatest good for the greatest number of people. Bobby may have to give up the opportunity for a government-funded experiment to return him to visible status in order to protect everyone else in society from the dangers that could result from discovering the science of invisibility. p. 220)*

8. Do you think Bobby is wise to sleep with his electric blanket again when he knows that the solar particle count is unusually high like it was the night he became invisible? *(Answers will vary. pp. 227–231)*

9. How do you think Bobby feels when he faces the officer in his room at 4:30 in the morning? *(Answers will vary. Note that, even though he has no clothes on and probably is embarrassed, Bobby can't help smiling because he is visible again. pp. 232–233)*

10. Sheila says she began disappearing before she became invisible. What does she mean? Do you think she has a reasonable argument for remaining invisible? Explain. *(Answers will vary. Suggestion: Sheila felt like she was disappearing because she was making poor life choices and neglecting to care for herself properly. Choosing to be around people who did not care for her and drinking or doing drugs was the way she tried to escape how she felt about herself. Eventually, such vices might have killed her or damaged her more. She is happy with her life as an invisible person and no longer falls back on those same vices to satisfy her desires or escape a poor self-image. Because of this, she chooses to continue living her life as an invisible person. She feels healthier now that she is invisible than when she was visible. pp. 238–239)*

11. During the course of the story, both Bobby and Alicia comment that years don't scare them anymore. What does this mean? What changes the way they feel about time? *(Answers will vary. Bobby and Alicia's perception of the world is much larger than it was before they faced their respective disabilities. Seeing the world from the vantage point of someone with limitations has shown them that there is more to life than the small world in which they live. They are eager to experience life, and having experience means more to them than the amount of time it takes to do something valuable. They are also willing to live as they are, accepting their specific circumstances and not worrying about when they might, if ever, change. pp. 230, 240)*

12. Alicia backs away from Bobby when he tries to kiss her. Later, she writes to him that she wants to make sure he sees her. What does she mean? Do you think Bobby "sees" her? *(Answers will vary. Suggestion: Alicia felt like she was disappearing before she met Bobby because everything about her former life had drifted away. She couldn't even see herself, and she couldn't imagine a future that included romance. When Bobby came along, he really got to know Alicia. Her blindness did not stop him from wanting to be with her or kiss her, and this scared her. Alicia wants Bobby to "see her" because she wants him to like her as she is, despite her flaws and disabilities. However, allowing others to "see us" is scary, as we risk being rejected if we are found imperfect or different from someone else's expectation of what we should be. pp. 245–251)*

Supplementary Activities

1. Figurative Language: Continue adding to your chart. Examples: **Similes**—"…Mom act like some tough guy" (p. 202); "[finding another invisible person is] like I'm finding a lost sister" (p. 205); "computer sounds like a diesel truck" (p. 223); "feel like a book being read, word by word" (p. 243); **Metaphors**—life of invisibility: prison (p. 240); Bobby: invisible mirror (p. 251); **Personification**—"eyes are devouring my face" (p. 235)

2. Art: On page 219, Bobby says he can read what his father and Dr. Van Dorn are thinking but not saying. Draw a picture of both men in which their expressions show what Bobby sees—that developing a workable theory will take a much longer time than they are willing to admit.

Post-reading Discussion Questions

1. Discuss how having the technology to make people invisible could change the way our society functions. Are all scientific discoveries beneficial to humankind, or are there some scientific questions people should not try to answer? *(Answers will vary.)*

2. Alicia felt rejected by most of her friends and peers after she became blind. What effect did that have on her? How does Bobby affect her? *(Answers will vary. Note that in her e-mail to Bobby at the end of the story, Alicia says she felt like she was disappearing. Bobby's attention to her makes her realize she still has something to offer and is still valuable as a person and a friend, regardless of her blindness. That Bobby dignifies her lets her believe that she is valuable and capable of living a full life.)*

3. What would you do if you could be invisible for a day? a month? *(Answers will vary. Help students recall how Bobby describes living with his invisibility as something that could exist forever versus something that is temporary.)*

4. Though he appreciates his parents, Bobby also experiences times of frustration with them. If you were Bobby's parents, would you have acted or treated Bobby differently in any part of the story? Explain. If you were Bobby, would you have treated Mr. and Mrs. Phillips differently? Explain. *(Answers will vary. Comment on the author's use of universalism with regard to the way Bobby and his parents interact. The author relates to his audience by describing a parental relationship that is not totally foreign from their own realities.)*

5. Discuss the role of Ms. Pagett in the novel. Why does the author include her character? Is her character believable? Is her character just? *(Answers will vary. Note that Ms. Pagett's presence in the novel adds tension to the plot line because she gives a time line by which Bobby must become visible. When looking at Bobby's disappearance from Ms. Pagett's perspective, it makes sense that she would search the Phillips home twice and try to find Aunt Ethel in Florida. As Bobby's father says near the end of the novel, she is doing her job, and Bobby's disappearance probably does look suspicious to her. Encourage students to consider whether they would have thought her actions just if a child really was missing due to a criminal act by the parents. The fact that Bobby is really not missing should not affect the way they evaluate Ms. Pagett's behavior.)*

6. Do you think Sheila will choose to make herself visible again after receiving the package from Bobby? Explain. *(Answers will vary.)*

7. Does Alicia's blindness or Bobby's invisibility change who they are as people? Explain. If you think it does not change them, explain why you think Alicia's friends avoided her after her accident. *(Answers will vary.)*

8. How does Bobby's relationship with his father change over the course of the novel? Explain. *(Answers will vary. Note that Bobby feels belittled and overlooked at the beginning of the story. His dad takes it upon himself to find the solution for Bobby's state. By the end of the book, Mr. Phillips shows more respect toward Bobby's efforts and is proud of the information Bobby gathers and the breakthroughs Bobby experiences. By the end, Bobby enjoys his father's attention and values the way his father feels about him. Bobby seems to enjoy being a participant in his father's life and study and not just someone his father feels he must teach.)*

9. Did you like the way the author incorporates other types of writing into his story, such as e-mails and instant messages? Why or why not? *(Answers will vary.)*

10. If you could change one part of the story, which part would you change and why? *(Answers will vary.)*

11. How would this story have been different in a world without the Internet, e-mail, or instant messages? *(Answers will vary. Note that Bobby uses the Internet to research about the SOHO experiment, to locate Sheila Borden, and to communicate with Alicia and his other friends.)*

12. Did you relate to any characters in the book? Explain. *(Answers will vary.)*

Post-reading Extension Activities

1. Imagine that the government and media found out about Bobby's invisibility. Write a headline and article that might appear on the front page of a prestigious newspaper reporting about Bobby Phillips and the impact of the science of invisibility on society.

2. Read and review one of the books referenced in the text, such as *The Scarlet Letter* by Nathaniel Hawthorne or *The Invisible Man* by H.G. Wells.

3. Draw a caricature of Ms. Pagett or Mrs. Trent.

4. Listen to an audio book like Alicia must do. Then write an essay that discusses the pros and cons of listening to stories as opposed to reading them on your own.

5. Pretend you are interviewing Bobby about his time as an invisible person. Write a transcript of the interview as you imagine it would go, listing your questions and Bobby's answers.

6. At the end of the story, Alicia writes an e-mail to Bobby explaining a little about how she feels about him. Write a poem from Bobby's point of view explaining how he feels about Alicia.

7. Make a collage that depicts either Bobby or Sheila. The collage should represent their lives as invisible people but can include references to the lives they had before they became invisible.

8. Conduct research on the history of jazz and famous jazz musicians, and explain why some people call it America's original art form.

9. Write a short story describing what Bobby and Alicia's first meeting would have been like if Alicia were not blind and Bobby were not invisible.

10. Write a short skit in which two people have a conversation in the presence of a third person who is invisible. Only one of the two people conversing knows the invisible person is present. Three people should then perform the skit for the class.

Assessment for *Things Not Seen*

Assessment is an ongoing process. The following ten items can be completed during the novel study. Once finished, the student and teacher will check the work. Points may be added to indicate the level of understanding.

Name _____ Date _____

Student	Teacher	
_____	_____	1. Complete at least two of the Post-reading Extension Activities and present one to the class.
_____	_____	2. List at least two conflicts that occur in the novel. Using a visual diagram, describe the conflict, identify what type of conflict it is, and explain how the conflict is resolved. If you would have resolved the conflict differently, also add your alternate form of resolution.
_____	_____	3. Complete the Character Web (see page 10 of this guide) for one of the characters in the novel.
_____	_____	4. Complete the Story Map (see page 11 of this guide) for the novel.
_____	_____	5. Complete the Cause/Effect Chart (see page 12 of this guide) for the novel.
_____	_____	6. Using the Venn Diagram on page 13 of this guide, make a list of the similarities and differences between Alicia and Bobby.
_____	_____	7. Rewrite the last chapter of the book in which Ms. Pagett and several police officers search the Phillips household at 4:30 a.m. In your version, have Bobby remain invisible.
_____	_____	8. Identify five major events that occur in the novel, and list them in sequential order. Then create or draw a symbol or image that describes each of the five events.
_____	_____	9. Write a review of the novel using at least 12 vocabulary words.
_____	_____	10. Correct any quizzes or exams taken over the novel.

Linking Novel Units® Lessons to National and State Reading Assessments

During the past several years, an increasing number of students have faced some form of state-mandated competency testing in reading. Many states now administer state-developed assessments to measure the skills and knowledge emphasized in their particular reading curriculum. The discussion questions and post-reading questions in this Novel Units® Teacher Guide make excellent open-ended comprehension questions and may be used throughout the daily lessons as practice activities. The rubric below provides important information for evaluating responses to open-ended comprehension questions. Teachers may also use scoring rubrics provided for their own state's competency test.

Please note: The Novel Units® Student Packet contains optional open-ended questions in a format similar to many national and state reading assessments.

Scoring Rubric for Open-Ended Items

3-Exemplary
Thorough, complete ideas/information
Clear organization throughout
Logical reasoning/conclusions
Thorough understanding of reading task
Accurate, complete response

2-Sufficient
Many relevant ideas/pieces of information
Clear organization throughout most of response
Minor problems in logical reasoning/conclusions
General understanding of reading task
Generally accurate and complete response

1-Partially Sufficient
Minimally relevant ideas/information
Obvious gaps in organization
Obvious problems in logical reasoning/conclusions
Minimal understanding of reading task
Inaccuracies/incomplete response

0-Insufficient
Irrelevant ideas/information
No coherent organization
Major problems in logical reasoning/conclusions
Little or no understanding of reading task
Generally inaccurate/incomplete response

Notes

Notes

© Novel Units, Inc.